MANAGING AND COPING WITH ANGER

"A Handbook of Proven Techniques"

By

Leonard Ingram

Royal House Publishing Co.

Royal House Publishing Co.
P.O. Box 4505-288
Oak Park, IL 60302
(312) 490-4301

Web Site: http://www.angermgmt.com

ISBN 1-893745-04-X

Edited by
Dorothy M. Johnson

Contents

Introduction

Anger happens to everybody, whether we openly express it or not. In America, however, we have been "culturally" conditioned, from childhood, to deny our anger. We were constantly told that "good" people do not get angry, that only "bad" or "crazy" people experience rage. Therefore, something must be "wrong" with *you!* We become convinced, at an early age, that "civilized" human beings do not get angry. As a result of this cultural myth, millions of Americans are in a deep state of denial when it comes to anger. We do not get angry. We get "annoyed," "irritated," "upset," and under extreme circumstances, occasionally "pissed off"—but *never* angry! That's too gross, too raw, too animalistic! We use these kinds of words as euphemisms to camouflage and cover up the reality of our raw anger, and we simply continue to deceive ourselves, and others, about our "suppressed" anger. This suppressed anger then becomes the source of conflict in our relationships with other people—both personally and professionally. Most of us are emotionally out of touch with ourselves when it comes to anger.

Anger is a natural, human emotion that is not racially, genetically, socio-economically, or gender based. And like any other emotion (feelings), such as joy, love, fear or hope, anger is a "subjective" interpretation of the human events and situations going on around us. In terms of its dynamics, anger is an emotional, physical, and mental response to the "perception" of an injustice, threat or attack on our personhood (grievance). The "threat" may be real or imaginary or past, present, or future, but if we "feel" we have been wronged; if we feel we have somehow been treated unfairly; we will *automatically* become angry. Anger is rooted in our "survival" instincts and has a legitimate and vital function in human behavior. The problem is *not* anger; the problem is the mismanagement of anger!

Unfortunately, because of our culture's deep state of denial in regard to anger, millions of Americans emerge from their upbringing and education "Emotionally Illiterate," with absolutely no skills enabling them to effectively manage their anger and rage in a nonviolent and psychologically healthy way. We are fully aware of the limitations that intellectual and academic "illiteracy" imposes on one's life, but few truly realize how crippled and impoverished their lives are due to their lack of skills for the appropriate management of their anger.

Anger is the specific emotion that underlies and sustains ALL violent and negative behavior! Violence, itself, is *not* an emotion or feeling. It is a negative and destructive *form of wrong behavior* we use as a means for handling anger. ALL SENSELESS VIOLENCE IS ROOTED IN MISMANAGED ANGER! Please make a note of it. Nobody is born violent; one learns it. One is "contaminated" by a violent society. When violence is all around the child, by and by, the child becomes violent. Otherwise, every child is born absolutely nonviolent.

Our cultural denial of anger and society's promotion of and preference for the violent resolution of conflicts (mismanaged anger) have created an epidemic level of homicide in this country. The United States has the highest murder rate in the world! Our citizens are so emotionally illiterate and unable to deal with their anger and frustration, nonviolently, that we now have the largest prison system in the world. It is also mismanaged anger that is destroying over 51% of ALL marriages in this country (80% when unconventional

Notes

relationships are factored in). It is mismanaged anger that lies at the core of all domestic violence, child abuse, date rape, random street crime, gang banging, substance abuse, work-site violence, and so on. It is mismanaged anger that fuels the twin social evils of racism and sexism. Indeed, it is the violence resulting from America's denial and mismanagement of its "cultural" anger that threatens to destroy the very foundation of Western civilization.

When this is the case, why are our politicians, educators, clergy, and even most parents, so reluctant to take this mismanaged anger as seriously as it needs to be taken? The reason is denial and ignorance. The damage that the violence of mismanaged anger is causing on a daily basis in this country is catastrophic, in both terms of dollars and the loss of human life. Violence has become a national epidemic across the land—so much so that the Center for Disease Control (CDC) has deemed it the single greatest threat to public health since polio. Random, senseless violence is a greater threat to public health than AIDS, especially in urban America. Among all urban dwellers ages 15-34, homicide is the *fourth* leading cause of death among White women; the *third* leading cause of death among White males; and the *single* leading cause of death for BOTH Black males and Black FEMALES! In fact, homicide is the third most common cause of death for urban Blacks regardless of age! Americans, of ALL races, creeds, and gender, are full of anger and rage, and whenever anger becomes too much, and emotional relief too little, the result is *always* violent and destructive. Anger, suppressed over time=rage=violence=crime=death=the destruction of Western civilization. The violence erupting from our "collective" denial and suppression of anger is maiming and killing us faster than any known disease!

We all live under a constant fear, not only for our lives, but also for the lives of our children. Who knows when someone—a co-worker, neighbor, or stranger—will *suddenly* explode into a violent act, destroying anyone who happens to be available. Urban America has become so saturated with these random acts of violence that over 45% of all inner-city children have witnessed at LEAST one (1) homicide *before* the age of SEVEN! Nightmares, poor concentration at school, lack of interest in outdoor activities, anxiety, fear, and emotional distance are just a few examples of the impact this random, casual killing is having on our children. In fact, post-traumatic stress syndrome is common among many inner-city youngsters. Indeed, we have all seen—some of us firsthand—the terrible consequences that the violence of mismanaged anger can, and often does, have on people's lives.

At the Anger Clinic and the House of Ra, we have also seen how quickly this damage can be repaired (even reversed) when people are given the right tools, and the right insights, for appropriately dealing with their anger and the anger of others. The need for the widespread dissemination of effective techniques and skills for managing anger is, I submit, most urgent.

Leonard Ingram
(Bhagwan Ra Afrika)

Chicago, Illinois

Notes

Part One

The Anatomy of Anger

The first step in managing our anger is to *admit* that we are angry. We can admit all kinds of other unpleasant things about ourselves, such as we are "too fat" or we "drink too much," but we have a problem admitting the existence of this "wild" emotion in our bosom. We must overcome our denial and "greet," "meet," and "defeat" this monster within us. In order to effectively manage your anger, you must gather the courage to look deeply into the nature of your anger. Rather than condemning it, rather than calling it by other names and giving it labels, investigate it. Look as deeply as possible into it—with deep intimacy. It is *your* anger. It says something about *you*; it is part of your biography. It has arisen from somewhere deep within your childhood, and you must clearly understand the emotional conditioning you have carried over from your childhood. You must become, or be made, aware of "What?" provokes and triggers your anger. You must begin to see how you have been "unconsciously" programmed to handle it.

Most of us have simply "mimicked" the emotional and psychological style(s) of our parents or others who influenced our early stages of development. If your Mom's style of "handling" her anger was to scream and curse, you might find that, as an adult, this is the same way you handle your anger. You have acquired that style of emotional behavior from your mother through psychological osmosis. Your Dad might have managed his anger by "kicking ass" and, as an adult, you find that you only know how to resolve conflicts with your fist. Or you may have mimicked an older brother, sister, aunt, or uncle, or any combination of the styles that were available to you during your formative stages of development. You get the point: Your style of managing your anger (as well as many other emotions) is not original; it is not based on your *own* insights. You are simply managing your anger the way you have seen others manage their anger. The problem, of course, is that they didn't know how to handle their anger either! So a legacy of emotional illiteracy is simply handed down to the next generation.

There is something like a "robot" part of the mind: Once you have "learned" to act a certain way, it is transferred to the robot part of your mind; then you continue to perform an action without your even being aware of it. You have been programmed to act a certain way. This is the one thing about human behavior that has to be deeply understood: we all were programmed during our childhood. A certain kind of program was put into your head and you are still following it. Your adult emotionality is full of these mechanical habits; you simply go on repeating them—and each generation passes these habits to the next.

When we are able to penetrate deeply into the psycho-historical origins of our "emotional and psychological styles" of handling our anger, we begin to see that anger, fundamentally, is triggered by the set of "attitudes" we formed toward life, others, and ourselves as children. As children, we developed all kinds of attitudes and opinions about life that were not true then and are not true now. Yet we still behave as if they were. In most instances, people are not even aware that these childish attitudes are still in them, silently influencing and controlling their adult behavior. Looking very deeply into the nature of our anger, we are now able to see and "*edit*" the mistaken conclusions we reached as children about life and

Notes

ourselves. We are now able to correct our attitudes using our adult intelligence and understanding.

I want to remind you that the problem is not anger; the problem is the mismanagement of anger. When we do not know how to manage this "anger energy" appropriately, we will manage it inappropriately every time. All violence, for instance, is rooted in anger. There can be no violence where there is no anger. Violence in any form—physical, emotional, financial, and intellectual—has to be rooted in anger. But what is anger itself more deeply rooted in? *Fear*. Whenever we have the sense of a threat to our well being, that frightens us at a deep level, and out of that state of fear, the anger energy arises to take some type of action to ward off that threat. We are not even conscious of it; it is happening beneath the threshold of our conscious mind.

With the completion of this initial investigation into the psychology of our anger, we are in a position to look at the biological and physiological aspects of our anger. Anger is a *bio-psyche* form of energy that impacts us across the entire spectrum of our being—body, mind, and soul. Therefore, in order to effectively manage our reaction to it, we must become aware of anger beginning at its grossest level—the body.

The Effects of Anger on the Body

In response to our anger, the body automatically and "instinctively" moves into an "optimum" state of readiness to prepare us, physically, to ward off our "perception" of a threat to our well being. *Anger energy* is nature's way of empowering us to effectively "fight" or "flee" the perceived danger. In response to anger, our body begins to secrete higher levels of adrenaline, release additional sugar, and pump nearly four times MORE blood to our muscles and brain! The digestive system, which uses the bulk of the body's supply of energy, is immediately arrested and its vast energy is shifted to the body's "defensive" system (fists, feet, etc.). Increased blood pressure, heart rate, and body temperature are additional bodily responses to our anger. Each process is designed to "maximize" our capacity to take some kind of physical action against the perceived threat. The reaction time between the "triggering" event (anger) and our physical "actions" is in MILLISECONDS! Once we become angry, we go off, *immediately*, "like a cheap pistol...." We react, far too fast to be monitored and controlled by the untrained, unskilled mass of humanity.

Or worst, in a misguided attempt to "hide" our anger, instead of resolving the conflict that triggered it, we "suppress" it. This pent-up energy creates pressure, tension, and stress throughout the entire body, causing all kinds of damage; i.e., migraine headaches, ulcers, high blood pressure, heart attacks, and even some forms of cancer! Make no mistake about it: mismanaged, suppressed anger can be fatal! The pain and anguish of this "unnatural" blocking of the flow of anger energy lies at the basis of most of our physical illnesses.

The Effects of Anger on the Mind

The psychological and functional impact of anger on the mind and its mental processes are, in many respects, even more drastic than its effect on the body! In fact, it is the most

Notes

primitive part of the mind-brain (the R-Complex) that houses our most basic survival instincts—including the capacity to *KILL* when provoked. This lower part of the mind-brain complex is the passageway through which the forces of primeval human nature shape the outcome of our mismanaged or "non-managed" anger. Man is still wild deep down inside his psyche. He has not lost his inner "affinity" with the beast; only on the surface does he look civilized. Civilization is a "conscious" effort, and whenever we lose conscious control of our anger, we fall immediately back to the level of an animal. We lose all sense of *self-control.* Nothing illustrates this descent into animality as dramatically as our uncontrolled and mismanaged anger.

When anger energy enters the mind zone, without conscious control, we "drop" down into "wild" mode, shutting down all rational thinking. Under the grip of mismanaged anger, we lose our capacity to think clearly. Unable to "think straight," we become "temporarily insane"! Access to our intelligence and wisdom, to our morality and character, is temporarily suspended and is replaced by a "blind" fury and rage. This is the "killing" mode of mind from which murder and all other "inhuman" acts by human beings arise. In fact, in this state of mind, many people are so angry they will even *warn* us, "...I'm so mad, I could kill somebody!" Unfortunately, too many hearers do not heed their warnings. All that is wrong and evil in mankind and womankind has its origin and roots deeply embedded in this "blind rage" mode of mind, and in order to effectively avoid this state of mind, we must ultimately develop the ability to "catch" ourselves BEFORE we drop down into it. We must stop anger before it reaches the level of the physical body.

When we get "trapped" in this state of Super Anger (rage), the emotional and psychological effects are devastating. Revenge, obsession, morbid depression, anxiety attacks, psychosis, and suicidal urges to kill begin to dominate the mind. The agony and sheer "hell" that characterizes this unfortunate state of mind is so painful and intense that, very often, the only relief available is the abuse of drugs, alcohol, food, sex, and so on. There can be no peace of mind where there is anger, especially Super Anger. Please make a note of it.

The Spiritual Effects of Anger

It is the *spiritual* part of man that enables us to have the higher experiences of love, joy beauty, and so on. When we mismanage our anger, we completely destroy the spiritual quality of our lives. We lose the capacity to have deep experiences of the joy and beauty that surrounds us. These "higher" experiences are generated through our spiritual faculty—the *Soul.* Our mismanaged anger envelopes the Soul in a "veil of darkness" and voids out all of these higher, spiritual experiences. In their place, mismanaged anger generates the opposite experiences. Where there was once love, anger creates fear; beauty is replaced with ugliness and cynicism; misery and pain replace joy and happiness. Life becomes bleak, meaningless, and cruel. It simply becomes a continuous struggle—an uninterrupted war between you and others; it is you against the world. By and by, your whole nature becomes poisoned by your hatred.

In this state of "chronic" anger, your intelligence begins to diminish and give way to an urge to fight, an urge to kill. In fact, you no longer even need any intelligence; it requires

Notes

NO intelligence to be angry and miserable! Of what use is it to you? Slowly, the mismanaged anger completely destroys your intellect and your capacity to "*understand*" life, to understand others—to even understand yourself! Eventually, your mismanaged anger creates a deep discord and disharmony between you and Reality. It destroys your ability to be in *Ma'at*—to live in harmony with others, with nature, with the world. You enter into a deep "conflict" with existence. Isolated, recoiling, withdrawn, you separate yourself from life, and this existential separation from life hurts. Peace of mind, joy, love, happiness, and ALL of the higher spiritual experiences available to human consciousness are possible ONLY if we know how to manage our anger appropriately. Less than this simply will not do!

The Tasks of Life

Before we begin to go into some of the specific arenas in life in which we are challenged to manage our anger, let us discuss the tasks of life we all must deal with as we emerge from our respective families of origin. Afterwards, you will be able to see clearly how managing the categories of anger will help you manage these tasks of life.

In our families of origin, our nuclear families, or whatever extended family we come out of, the idea is to prepare us for the outside world in very specific ways. If we fail to learn those skills within the context of our upbringing, then it stands to reason that in the real world we are going to have some problems. All of us came from some sort of family, and our mothers and fathers were probably no more perfect than we are, and we know we are not perfect. So, obviously, they made some mistakes. The problem, of course, is that the effects of these mistakes are buried very deep within our psyche and our unconscious, and very often are what drive our adult behavior. Most of us have never developed enough subjective sensitivity to see our own conditioning. In fact, we do not even think we are conditioned! We think we are making decisions that are spontaneous and reflective of the situations. However, most of our reactions are triggered from that deep part of us and we have no idea of the depth of our conditioning. Thus, we need to get in touch with that.

Livelihood

In any case, when we emerge from these family systems, there are certain tasks of life we have to confront and negotiate in our adult life. The first one is our work, our livelihood. When we come out of the family system, we must be able to make a living, and very often if we have not been prepared, then we will have trouble. When I say have a livelihood, I do not mean simply get a job, because the work you do is probably as important as who you marry. That may sound strange to you, but I am telling you that the work you do, the way you make a living, plays a tremendous role in your body-mind experience of happiness. Hence, if you are working eight and nine hours a day on a job you hate, half of your life is spent in a state of hate and anger! You have lost half of the opportunity to be happy in the course of the day just by going to work. It's deep! Thus, you must find the right livelihood. I want to emphasize that: the *right livelihood*.

It means work that you love, work in which you are making a contribution. Work that you love, you tend to be very successful in. All the things you are looking for, you will get

Notes

automatically; it is a byproduct. The problem is that most of us are so out of touch with who we are that we do not know what we want to do. We do not have enough *self-knowledge*. We are just doing whatever will pay the most or that society says to do. It is almost like you just married whom society said you should marry. It is the same kind of irrational approach toward life as choosing the wrong work. We do not know the intimate relationship our work has with our happiness and peace of mind. Nevertheless, as we emerge from the process of being reared and enter into the "real" world, we must have developed the skills to find the right livelihood.

Love

The second task is love. We all are trying to be loved and to love. We do not have a choice; it is built into the structure of consciousness. We have no option, just like we have to breathe. You can fight it, you can hold your breath, but you cannot kill yourself by holding your breath. Nature will force you to breathe. In the same way, you must find some trick, like holding your nose, to deny love. You may even get your friends together to talk you out of going with this man or this woman! The point is that you have to be able to get your love needs met. Your family was just dumped on you. Your parents loved you simply because you were theirs; it did not require you to do anything. You then started expecting the whole world to give you that same love and affection. We grow up very childish, and very often project that same expectation onto people that we meet in our adult life.

If my mother has indiscriminately and unconditionally loved me, that love has a certain pattern that is unique to the relationship I have with her. It feels good because it is unconditional. Then I get married and will instantly project onto my wife that same expectation, although I am not conscious of it. The difference is that she is not my mother! I cannot say, "Okay, love me because I put a ring on your finger." This is madness! So we have to develop those skills that will enable us to have the experience in life called love, because life without love is meaningless! One of the great tragedies of the modern world, particularly Western society, is that somehow we have bought the bankrupt notion that life can be worth living without love. Lots of people with money and great careers have blown their brains out.

We have the potential to love, but often do not have the skills to implement it. Again, our ego myths get in the way, because we do not want to be vulnerable. We do not want to be at risk. We want to protect ourselves and curl up, but we cannot experience love all curled up. It means we have to be able to walk into the situation with every possibility of heartbreak. Yes, it can go either way, but that risk must be there in order to have the experience of love. Most of us do not have the ability to manage ourselves that way. It is very hard, because the instinct to withdraw, to avoid, is there, and great skill is required to pull us out of that. In Buddhism they call it "skillful means." So there is a skill in how to love. Everybody is born with the potential to love, but very few develop the ability and skills to love.

Love is a very rare phenomenon, though you would think otherwise. There are billions of us running around interacting with each other, but love is very rare. My definition of love is very different from the "business" relationships most of us have. What most of us call "love" is business: "I'll do this for you, wife."; "Be a good husband, and I'll do this in return

Notes

for you. But if you don't do this, I'm not going to do anything!" That's business. There is nothing wrong with it; sign a contract and be clear on the matter, but do not call that "love." It does not look like love to anybody who has seen love.

It is easy to have a business relationship with another person and disguise that as love, but it is just business. Love is when you are trying to give something. It is characterized by the fact that it is a gift. It is not looking for anything in return. Hence, we use a mother's love for a child as the closest analogy we have for talking about the authentic thing, because a mother's love for her child is really quite a phenomenon, isn't it? That kind of love is totally unconditional: it looks for nothing in return. It is a one-way street, so to speak, and the beloved is a great opportunity to unload your love. Let me put it to you in very strong terms. Most of the emotional misery that underlies the insanity and emotional illness we see plaguing people is the result of their efforts to suppress love. We are talking about suppressing anger and how damaging that is. Suppressing anger is just going to wipe out your mind; suppress love and you will lose your Soul!

You cannot suppress it on either side, as giver or recipient. Unfortunately, we try to suppress it on both sides: "I don't need any love and I don't love nobody!" That's almost the American battle cry. "I don't love nobody and I don't need anybody to love me. Just give me some money! What's love got to do with it?" Madness! Look at the people who are following that philosophy. Their lives are horrendous. So we have to develop the ability to move outside of the confinements generated by this ego-mythology. We have to learn the skills to drop this ego. Most of us do not know how to drop the ego. It is very hard, in fact, but we have to learn that, presumably ideally in the context of a family. Of course, that is rare and almost nonexistent today.

The ego is our felt sense of distinctiveness and separateness. When this sense of separateness or distinctness becomes a sense of "disconnectedness," then we enter into trouble, because the reality is that everything is connected. We live in an ecosystem. At the deepest level of our being, we are all connected. That is what psychologists call the "unknown," the true unconscious. It is unconscious because you cannot "know" it, not through any intellectual process. You have to "experience" it, the God, the Divine, the Creator, the collective unconscious "something" that is in all of us. The ego—when it is mismanaged and out of control—gives one the illusion that one is disconnected from the rest of creation, and that is where all our fears start. We start slipping into this radical individualism because we are alone. It is "me" against the world. We *cannot* love or be loved in that state.

Cooperation

The third thing we have to develop is the skill to cooperate. We must have cooperative skills because, again, we are all interdependent. None of us in here could survive independently of everybody else. You cannot farm all the food you eat; most of us are not making the clothes and shoes we wear and the gears in our cars. Our whole existence is dependent upon some other human being producing something, and we therefore have to learn how to cooperate. This radical individualism of "I can do my own thing" does *not* work! It is not even real. So we have to develop skills to enable us to cooperate and develop

Notes

friendships. Otherwise, we will move through life full of competition and with no friends. It is an ugly thing to see a human being reduced to being totally competitive and friendless!

Relationship to Self (Self-respect)

The fourth task is your relationship to yourself. That is very, very important because no matter how hard you try, you are not going to have successful relationships with other people if you do not first have a successful relationship with yourself. You do not even know who you are, so how can you have a self-relationship? Hence, again, the first step is knowing who you are. Most of us do not know who we are, and therefore have no relationship with ourselves. We are alienated from our own life. One of the poets said that the greatest tragedy that can befall a person is to have lived his whole life and have been absent the whole time. That absence is experienced as a deep sense of a lack of fulfillment. Nothing you are doing is giving you any fulfillment. You have tried this, you have tried that; you married him, you married her; you bought this, you bought that; and nothing fills that void, that abyss, inside you. That is because you are absent from your own life, and when you are absent from your own life, that life is meaningless. The price you pay is one of uninterrupted misery and suffering. Thoreau wrote that men (and women) are leading lives of "quiet desperation." Underneath all that pretty makeup, the beautiful haircuts, and stylish clothes, are pain and suffering, hopelessness and bleakness. There is no relationship with the Self. So we have to develop a relationship with ourselves, and the most important aspect of that relationship with the Self is self-respect.

I make a very big distinction between "self-respect" and "self-esteem." Esteem means estimate, and comes from the same root word as estimation. It is our estimation of ourselves. It is made of the same stuff that dreams are made out of. Our self-esteem is our propaganda, our mythology, stuff we created about ourselves that has no reality at all! Self-respect is a very different relationship with oneself. Self-respect is based on the realization that, "I have imperfections, I have faults, I have shortcomings and, in spite of those imperfections, shortcomings, and faults, I have value and worth as a human being." Case is closed! There is nothing to debate about that. "I exist, therefore, I have value." Period! The moment that anything (or anyone) ceases to exist, only then can it be said to be worthless, because nature or existence does not maintain anything that does not have value and worth. The very fact that we exist means we have worth and value. Self-respect is not just the understanding of that, it is the *feeling*. Self-esteem is a cerebral phenomenon; it has to do with your philosophy. Self-respect is a felt experience; you feel it in the same place as you feel love. It permeates your whole being.

We must develop a relationship of self-respect, not self-delusion or self-deception, because at some point in all of our lives all of our self-deceptions dissolve. Life is going to bring us those experiences where all of that mythology we had about ourselves—"I'm intelligent, I'm loving, I'm compassionate, I'm honest, I'm fair, I'm brilliant"—is going to be totally dissolved. You are going to be left in a mid-life crisis that will be hell. It has been my observation that very few people enter the mid-life crisis and emerge. Most people perish in that cycle, because few of us have any concept of how to get out of it. It is inevitable, because all of that imaginary, magical thinking from your childhood, from the time you thought you could fly through windows, has followed you into your adulthood. Now you

Notes

think, "I can make $20 million." This is magical thinking that has carried over from somewhere in your childhood, and it is causing you all kinds of misery because you keep failing to make the $20 million and, therefore, are experiencing shame in your own eyes. Then you sink into that depression, all because you were attempting to live life through the mind of a child, which was a kind of "Superman" complex.

We have to develop a very different relationship with ourselves predicated on the fact that we *all* have imperfections, shortcomings, and faults, with no exceptions, and there is nothing wrong with that. We will discover them and work on them, but in the meantime, our value and worth as a human being is unquestioned. You do not need a Ph.D. to be valuable. You have been told that unless you get a Ph.D., you are nobody. Unless you go to Harvard, you are nobody. Unless you buy a big house, you are nobody. You have been fed this stuff so long that now you have this deep sense that, "My God, without these things, I *am* nobody." But you were *somebody* when you hit the planet! Nothing else is required but for you to celebrate it. Life is a celebration! You made it. This *is* the graduation. This is the top of the rung. Folks, this human body is the big time. On this planet there are 8,400,000 other bodies you have been through to get to this human body. Who knows how long it has taken you to get here? You have paid all the dues. There is no preparation. You do not have to be anybody. You already *are*. Nobody says to a tree, "Tree, be somebody." You *be*! What is there to be?

Our whole identity or sense of worth is based on having more. We have that "have more" mentality. Just be more of yourself. That is all you have to do. Why? Because God has implanted in each and every thing in creation an aspect of His uniqueness, His greatness, His grandness. God *is* the sum total of that which exists, and in each article of that which exists is a reflection of the immensity of the phenomenon called "God." Unique! Not repeated at all. Hence, you are endowed—by virtue of the fact that you exist—with a quality of God that is in nobody else. If you fail to unfold that and share it with creation, then you have cheated all of us and have betrayed your own gift. Just be more of what you already are, as opposed to this "have more" in order to be "somebody."

Again, these are shifts in one's relationship with oneself, and that has to occur. If you have not tried to first improve your relationship with *yourself*, there is no sense in trying to improve your relationship with your spouse, or your children, or your boss, or your friends. In what area of the relationship are you trying to work, if you have not first worked on improving your relationship with yourself? If you have not accepted yourself, why should anybody else accept you? That is why you are trying to get all of these accouterments, because deep down inside you feel that, as you are, you are inadequate. So, "Let me get two Ph.D.s. Let me get four Mercedes Benzes. Let me get seven houses. Because then maybe...." That is nonsense!

Deep down inside you feel inferior. Deep down inside you feel you have no value and worth, naked, just as you are. I am telling you that, just as you are, you have worth enough. You *cannot* have more worth than that. In fact, this other stuff *obscures* your worth. I cannot see your value beyond all of those Mercedes Benzes. The Mercedes Benzes blind us. Those Ph.D.s have blinded your natural intelligence. I could see your brilliance clearly if there were no Ph.D.s. But you went and got those Ph.D.s, so now I think, "Well, maybe he is brilliant because he has a Ph.D.," not realizing you were brilliant *before* the Ph.D.

Notes

Sometimes these things obscure the fact, and we must not lose ourselves, our identities, in them.

Again, we must alter our relationship with ourselves, and very rarely does anyone tell us this when we are growing up. Your Mama said, "If you don't get yourself a job and a car and get out of here, you are going to be nothing!" She does not know any better, but when you are telling that to a four- or five-year-old child who believes the parent is infallible, who believes it when the parent says there is a Santa, the child buys it lock, stock and barrel. It is what Bilal (Bhagwan's brother) calls "the age of wonder and magic." When that parent tells the child, "You are not going to be anything, unless you do this, this and this," the child spends his whole life struggling, trying to be somebody. Thus, we have to restore the right relationship to ourselves, which necessitates a lot of work on oneself.

Mortality

The fifth, and certainly not the least, task we have to be prepared for is our own *mortality*. Death is real, certain; we can count on it! Now we have to find some means of taking death into consideration, because why are you struggling to pay your mortgage off? You are talking about a little 30 or 40 years. You have a life-span of about 70 years on this little planet called Earth, a little speck of mud floating amidst the appalling immensity of the physical universe. You are down on this little piece of mud, in this neighborhood for 70 years, and what are 70 years of life out of eternity? It is nothing! Death is *real*, and life has to remain meaningful within the context of death.

We do the opposite: in our culture we hide from death. All the cemeteries are put out on the edge of town. Everything is hidden. Nobody sees it, so we can live in denial of death. In fact, you see everybody else dying, but you never see *yourself* dying. Now, this is strange. You see everybody dying, but for some reason you think *you* are not going to die, and the reality is that you are going to *die*. You have to deal with your mortality and, if you do not, believe me, you will experience a crisis at about 35 or 40. Suddenly, the body is going to start breaking down, the eyes will begin to go bad, and you will realize, "My God, I'm going to die."

It hits you at mid-life and, again, one of things I have noticed during the mid-life crisis is that there are so few of us prepared for the inevitability of our own demise. It shakes us up. That is one of the first delusions that start dissolving. So we have to prepare ourselves. We have to live a life that is so authentic that when death comes, "I'm not going to have anything left for it to take. I have used up all my life. Take these bones and this bag of skin. I have spent all my life." But when you have held back living, thinking that you are not going to die, when death comes—and it will come—you will cling and scream and beg for one more hour: "Give me one more hour so I can get that Mercedes. Give me more time so I can get that house." Full of regret, you will die like a coward. People like that die a billion times in one life. A "real" person dies once. It is over with, because you have lived abundantly, fully. That is what the scriptures mean, that we have been given life abundantly. You live it!

When I say "death," I do not mean your Soul, your consciousness. When I talk about mortality, I'm talking about your ego, because you have been dead people before. The consciousness that makes up this configuration, this entity or person that I call "Bhagwan,"

Notes

has existed before, and it will go on existing. The body will change, yes. The little ego will change, of course. But if you are identified with the ego and the body, then you will experience death. If your identity has been shifted to the deepest recesses of your being, to where Jesus, Lord Krishna, and the Buddha shifted theirs, then you know you do not die. What is the problem? There *is* no problem. It is a very different thing. Again, seeing or preparing for our mortality necessitates the shift of the level of our identity off this body and this ego. Otherwise, we will live under the fear and tyranny of death, and you cannot live like that. You cannot live if you are afraid of death. It is not possible. These, then, are the tasks that we need to be prepared for in order to make the most of our adult lives.

Notes

Part Two

The Five Objects of Anger

Modern life is filled with events and situations that challenge us all to deal with some aspect of anger every *twelve seconds*! Whether it is our anger at others, or others' anger at us, how we manage the conflict is of utmost importance. Conflict between human beings is inevitable. There is no such thing as "conflict-free" human relationships. Each of us brings a different childhood conditioning into our relationships that is bound to contain values, attitudes, and "emotional" styles that are not the same. Our attempt to eliminate the conflict inherent in human interactions is to attempt the impossible. Our goal is to acquire the necessary skill to be able to "resolve" our conflicts with others in a nonviolent and psychologically healthy way. Unfortunately, the vast majority of us are inadequately prepared to deal effectively with the incidents of anger we will inevitably encounter in our everyday life. Most of the techniques we use to manage our day-to-day conflicts with others are no more than the carryover of the SAME way we handled conflicts as children.

The sad reality is that, EMOTIONALLY, most of us are still children. This is seen most clearly in the way we handle our anger and our conflicts with others. "Sulking," the "silent treatment;" "fighting," "revenge," "sarcasm," "banging walls," "self-mutilation," as well as many other ways we deal with our anger and conflicts, are ineffective and clearly childish. None of these ways will work in the adult world. The first step toward developing more effective and "appropriate" skills for managing our anger is overcoming these old routines rooted in our childhood—emotional and psychological styles that we never outgrew.

Effective anger management begins with us identifying these old childhood patterns and "catching" ourselves in the act of following them. In short, we must increase our "self-awareness." With practice, we will eventually be able to more frequently catch these childish "reactions" and replace them with more adult and appropriate behavior. Hence, self-observation is the foundation for developing effective skills to manage anger and conflicts. Next, we must become fully "aware" of the object(s) of our anger.

There are five major categories or objects of anger. The first is our anger at others; the second is others' anger at us; the third is our anger at self; the fourth is anger at the absent other; and the fifth is abstract or cosmic anger.

Object #1 — Managing Our Anger at Others

The biggest failures in the world are people who CANNOT resolve their conflicts with other people nonviolently and appropriately. They will suffer in a hundred and one ways because each of our lives is *inseparably* CONNECTED to hundreds of OTHER lives. For the person with no skill or ability to manage his anger at others effectively, the "others" will always be a problem for him. There will always be a battle between him and the others to dominate each other. Each human being has his or her own vision of life, his or her own ambitions. The "others" we are connected to have their own dreams of how they want their lives to unfold. That is not the problem; the problem is that their dreams and ambitions are bound to "clash" with YOURS! Their dreams and hopes cannot be "exactly" the same as

Notes

yours because each individual is unique. Hence, the inevitability of conflict is inherent in ALL human relationships.

Whenever you have the "perception" that someone is violating YOUR concept of what is important; of what is right or wrong; of what "should" or "should not" be; or what is or is not FAIR, you get angry at them. You FEEL they are trying to "sabotage" *your* hopes, *your* dreams, and *your* ambitions. This mismanaged anger will pit husband against wife and push them to the brink of divorce and, ultimately, over the edge. This mismanaged anger will disrupt and destroy life-long friendships, alienate children from parents, and completely destroy business partnerships. Ultimately, it plunges us into depression and utter despair.

Please remember that, *usually,* the precipitating event of your anger at the other is simply *YOUR* childish response and reaction to adult reality. Fundamentally, the majority of the anger we have at other people occurs whenever we CAN'T GET OUR OWN WAY! We very often try to "dress" our selfishness up in logic and reason; however, the bottom line is still to somehow get our own way. When we cannot, we get angry. To expect to always get your way with other people is egocentric, infantile, and completely out of sync with adult reality. As long as you remain the prisoner of the emotional *attitudes* of a four-year-old child, your conflicts with other people will only escalate. This kind of childish attitude is bound to result in a state of continuous anger; a state of *"chronic"* anger, completely destroying your relationships with other people.

Trapped in this kind of "selfish" mind-set, you will not be able to elicit the "cooperation" of other people in the fulfillment of your dreams and ambitions, and the ability and skill to secure others' help is the key to any form of success. When you cannot manage your anger at others, nonviolently and appropriately, you destroy their willingness to cooperate and help you achieve your goals of life. For example, if you do not know how to manage your anger at your boss or an employee or co-worker, you are going to have a hard time holding a job or retaining employees.

Take a moment, RIGHT NOW, and make a thorough list of those things that "trigger" your anger at other people? What things make you the "most" angry? When you are treated unfairly? When you feel powerless and out of control? When you feel unappreciated or abandoned? When you feel defeated or inferior?

Look deeply into the nature of your anger and try to see what fundamental sets of "attitudes" your triggers are rooted in. Are these *"root"* conclusions about life, your attitudes toward others and yourself TRUE? WHO are you the most angry at? What happened to make you so angry? Were you "angrier" than the situation warranted? What makes you the MOST angry about what happened? Examine your anger in detail, focusing on the underlying feelings that go through your mind. After a little practice of these "mental" exercises, a deeper insight into the "unconscious" processes governing your anger reactions is realized and understood, making it possible to effectively manage your anger. We must take advantage of every opportunity to "consciously" change our way of responding to conflicts by "choosing" to behave more *intelligently* and wisely. Replacing our old childish reactions and attitudes with new ones is what we shall mean by *"Homework."*

Notes

Homework #1: Tell the truth!

Most of us consider ourselves to be honest people who usually tell the truth. Of course, it is EASY to tell the truth when there is NOTHING at stake! However, what about our telling the truth when THERE IS? When we are angry at the boss, we would be able to give ourselves some emotional relief by telling the boss how angry we are. That would be telling the truth. But we are in such deep denial about our anger at others, so afraid of the consequences, that we automatically "suppress" our anger at the boss. We suppress our legitimate anger in order to keep from provoking a dangerous counterreaction. Instead of confronting our boss, we go home and "displace" our suppressed anger and rage on our innocent family and friends. This is simply the act of a coward.

It takes real COURAGE to tell the truth. That's why most of us cannot do it, especially when there is something REAL (your job) at stake. But if you can take the "risk" and tell the truth when you are angry at others, no matter how "important" they are, and do it "appropriately" (in such a way as to NOT trigger their anger), the truth "shall set YOU free!" Free of what? Free of your ANGER! Free of the anguish and agony of your suppressed rage.

Instead of waiting for people to "understand," we can tell the truth right away: "It makes me angry when you do such and such a thing." People CANNOT read your mind! How else will they know about your grievance against them if you don't tell the truth about how they make you feel? Where is the opportunity for them to participate in the resolution of the conflict? By using your adult intelligence and good judgment, you give yourself the choice to tell the other person the truth or to let it pass. But under no circumstances (i.e., fear) are you going to "suppress" your feeling of anger and make yourself, and everyone else around you, sick! Emotionally mature individuals are able to recognize what the "reality" of their situations requires them to do, and then do it. Their judgment need not be perfect, just good enough.

Homework #2: Validate Yourself

One of the major reasons we get angry at others is because their actions make us feel inferior and "worthless." Our sense of worthlessness (self-contempt) arises from our attempt to live our lives on other people's "terms." Very often, we don't even know what those terms are! We try to keep people from hurting us by being "pleasing." When we are trapped in the "*Pleaser Syndrome*" and are not even sure "what" we should be doing with our lives in order to please the "other," we become very confused and FRUSTRATED. In this *confused* state of mind, we try to suppress our anger and frustration until it reaches a point where we can suppress it no longer, and then we "explode." And the cycle simply starts all over again: we continue to seek others' "validation" of our worth and value as a human being. By learning how to validate our own self and live on our OWN terms, we are able to break this vicious cycle.

When you refuse to live on your own terms and depend on other people to validate you, your whole sense of value and worth as a human being is in the hands of *other* people— people over whom you have ABSOLUTELY no control. You have abdicated your own autonomy and authority. Hence, you lose the capacity and "freedom" to be "yourself." You

Notes

are no longer authentic; you become "absent" from your own life. Whether you like it or not does not matter to you. The whole question is whether OTHERS like it! If they want you to smile, you smile. The smile itself may be phony, but that is not the point—the point is whether THEY liked it. Unconsciously, nobody likes being dependent and enslaved. Anyone who becomes "emotionally" dependent on somebody else will "secretly" hate (suppressed anger!) that person. Even though the anger and hatred is hidden behind a beautiful garb of love and obedience, sooner or later, it is bound to emerge and take FULL revenge. The only antidote for this desperate state of mind is to develop some self-respect.

Self-respect, the feeling of being worthwhile and valuable IN SPITE of our imperfections, shortcomings, and faults, is a powerful antidote for "diffusing" our anger at others. As previously stated, self-respect is a very different phenomenon from high self-esteem. High self-esteem is our "estimation" of ourselves. It is our opinion "about" ourselves that we create. It is a pseudo phenomenon made up of the same stuff that dreams are made out of. It is the "image" we present to other people somehow hoping to "convince" them of our worth and value. It is a "political" construct designed to win us popularity, admiration, and social acceptance. We simply arrogate to ourselves qualities and virtues that we, in reality, DO NOT "truly" possess. When our estimation of self-worth is based on false premises, mistaken reasoning, or our parents over-indulging us as children, what worth is it? It is worth nothing! It is simply a *myth: a fairy tale we have created about ourselves*—ego-mythology.

These kinds of individuals can be seen swaggering and "strutting" around everywhere you go. They are suffering from severe *ego-mythology*, a kind of "false self-esteem" mental disorder. It is simply *arrogance* and bravado, and their conscious attempt to *hide* their imperfections, shortcomings, and faults from others—and even from themselves! Their self-esteem is a by-product of their "false egos." Self-respect is a concrete "experience" of actually being a worthwhile human being, which includes an *active* awareness of our shortcomings and imperfections. Doing our "homework" on ourselves leads, automatically, to the development of more and more self-respect.

Homework #3: Forgiving Others

Learning to forgive others is another very powerful and very effective means of diffusing our anger at others. Yet, for most of us, it is a very difficult task to *forgive* "those who have trespassed against you...." Why? Very often, it is our "mis-definition" and misunderstanding of what it means to forgive others that impedes our efforts. In the absence of a TRUE understanding of what forgiving others means, we simply withhold it out of fear and *spiritual ignorance*. To forgive is not the same as "condoning" or "legitimizing" the other's behavior. To forgive is an act that we do IN OUR OWN BEHALF! It is a kind of "emotional first aid" we give ourselves in order to get relief from OUR anger. It is MY anger that is causing me to suffer. I AM the one who is full of anguish and agony. To forgive the other person is a means of letting go of MY OWN anger and, thus, letting go of MY agony. It is my CONSCIOUS and DELIBERATE choice to stop "clinging" to my resentment of being done wrong. It has NOTHING directly to do with the other person. In fact, the other person need not even KNOW we have forgiven them. To forgive is completely subjective. It is between me, myself, and I.

Notes

To forgive the other simply means you adapt to the "reality" of who and what they are. You are no longer interested in "editing" them; you choose to be nonjudgmental. Ordinarily, we think "knowing" or "proving" that the other person did something "wrong" and then letting it go is what forgiving means. First you judge them, and then you forgive them. No, this kind of forgiveness is false, pseudo, and will not give you any real or lasting relief from your anger. Real, authentic forgiveness contains no judgment component. It never says, "You have done something very bad and wrong, but still I will forgive you...." It simply adapts and adjusts to the person as they REALLY are. It is completely based on reality. It is an existential response to the "truth." There is no "grudge," no complaint, no grumbling. When this understanding becomes deep, there is no longer even a question of "forgiving" them. There will be no anger. The pressure, tension, and agony of anger have simply disappeared into thin air. Only the calmness of this pure understanding remains. You then know you have done your homework right. Absolutely right.

Homework #4: Practicing Emotional Awareness

All acts flowing out of our mismanaged anger at others are self-defeating and, ultimately, counterproductive. Our out-of-control anger affects everything we do. In a state of anger, a deep undercurrent of madness permeates everything we do. In fact, in such a state of "madness," everything we do or say will be wrong. We were "unaware" of a sudden "anger attack" coming on, and we then find ourselves being swept away in a blind and raging fury, destroying everyone and everything crossing our path and, very often, even destroying ourselves. These sudden eruptions of anger can be successfully overcome by the practice of "watching" our mind.

The miracle of practicing "emotional" awareness is that you need not do anything except become more and more aware. Automatically, you are able to transform your anger! In fact, it is not even right to say you are doing something, because you really did not do anything. You only need to be a little patient. Try it: When anger comes again, don't do anything; just sit silently and watch it. Keep your eyes on it. Don't take sides; don't be for it or against it. Don't fan it nor suppress it; don't repress it. Just WATCH it. Be a little patient and just see what happens. This very phenomenon of watching the mind, when mastered, protects us from these random eruptions of anger. In fact, everybody becomes aware of their destructive, anger-driven actions, but only when the act is finished! You become angry— you slapped your wife or you threw a vase at your husband—and later on when you have cooled down and the anger has passed, you become aware of the damage. However, now it is too late; the damage that has been done cannot be undone. Yet the anger was already there, inside of you, like smoke, *before* the damage was done.

There are three stages in the practice of emotional awareness, and it is essential for you to understand each one. Becoming aware of your anger in the very midst of the act is the first level of the practice. It is difficult, but not impossible. With just a little more effort you will be able to "catch" your anger in the act. In the beginning you will still notice yourself becoming aware of the anger attack only *after* everything has cooled down, perhaps half an hour or an hour later. Continue practicing and you will then become aware after just fifteen minutes. Try a little more, and you will become aware in just one minute, immediately as the anger begins to evaporate. Keep practicing, and you will become aware exactly in the

Notes

middle of the act! This is the first level of mastery: to become aware of your anger IN THE ACT.

The second level of the practice of emotional awareness is a little more difficult because now we are moving into deeper water. The second level involves becoming aware of your anger BEFORE the act—when the act has not yet happened and is still just a thought! It has not been actualized but has become a thought in your mind. It is there, potentially, like a seed; it can become an action at any moment. To master this second level of the practice—to catch hold of the "angry thoughts" themselves as they arise in you—requires a more subtle degree of awareness. Please remember that this is not the same thing as suppressing your thoughts. "*Suppression*" is an act of mismanaging anger. *Catching* the thoughts can be done, but it can be done only AFTER you have mastered the first level of the practice, because your thoughts are not so solid as your physical behavior. However, they are solid enough to be "seen"; you just have to practice a little harder.

When a thought is moving in your mind, just watch it—and suddenly you will "see" that the thought is there and that you are somewhere else. There is a distance, a kind of "inner" space between you and it. And then, very slowly, you see an inner traffic of thousands of thoughts, dreams, and desires passing by. Just watch them as somebody sitting on the riverbank watches the tides go by. Just by watching them, you will become aware that you are NOT your thoughts! You will become "dis-identified" with them and will no longer be "possessed" by them.

The third level of the practice is to finally catch hold of the actual "process" that transforms these thoughts into actions! This is the subtlest and most difficult step, but if you can become aware of your thoughts, then it is just one step more. Just a little more intensity of awareness is needed.

To catch your anger even before it becomes a thought is, indeed, most difficult. Right now, you cannot even conceive of it! Before anger takes the form of thoughts, it is an "impulse." You may not be aware that each thought is produced by a certain emotional impulse; an "emotional ground" ... a "mood." Notice how sometimes you are feeling a little disturbed. You really don't know why: there seems to be no *real* reason for it. No cluster of brooding thoughts or outside event seems to be related to the feeling, but still you *FEEL* disturbed. Something is going on underground. Your anger is gathering force. If you are able to become aware of your angry thoughts prior to your anger reactions, you will—with more practice—ultimately become aware of the nuances of these underground impulses. These are the three levels of the practice. The *key* to success for this homework is practice, more practice, and MORE PRACTICE!

Object #2 — Managing the Other's Anger at You

"The other is hell...," writes Jean Paul Sartre. But, then, who are *you*? For other people, YOU are hell! You are the source of their conflict; the source of their agony and misery. First, look deeply into the real nature of your relationship and connection with other people. Any effective management of others' anger at you MUST be rooted in the understanding of this reality. Please be reminded that the mismanagement of the other's anger at you can be fatal. According to a recent morbidity and mortality report published by the Center for

Notes

Disease Control (CDC), over 60% of all homicides stemming from conflicts not associated with a crime involved victims who were KILLED by a family member or friend! This means that you are MORE likely to be murdered by an angry family member or friend than you are by a criminal! The appropriate and effective management of the other's anger at you is, therefore, essential. Your very life may one day depend upon it. Judging by the numbers of these kinds of homicides occurring every day in our society, most of us do not know how to handle this problem. How are you handling the anger of others at you? Are you simply setting yourself up "...for the kill"?

The greatest impediment to effectively managing others' anger at us is the illusion of our own "perfection." It is our lack of "humility" and realization of our own imperfections, faults, and shortcomings that makes handling the other's anger at us so painful and difficult. Full of self-deception and groundless vanity, we find it hard to believe that we are the "real" source of someone's grievance; that they are not simply "tripping." Instead, we think if they are angry at us, they must be crazy! *How can anyone become angry with someone as good and as perfect as I am?*

Homework #5: Do Not Take it Personally

When someone becomes angry at us, their anger creates a problem for our false ego. It threatens to destroy our "ego-mythology," the false image of ourselves that we have been working hard to maintain our whole life. Our first instinct is to "defend" our exaggerated and imaginary perfection, to somehow protect our "nice guy" image from total annihilation. Individuals who suffer from a lack of self-respect are very vulnerable to taking others' angry remarks toward them very personal. We take the other's angry words to us literally, and feeling threatened by their anger, we seek to defend ourselves against the *"pains of imperfection"* by going on the counteroffensive. Reacting to the other's *negative remarks* about us as if they are a reflection of our value and worth as a human being, we go into "overdrive" to defend ourselves against this perceived "attack" on our personhood. We launch our own counterattack at the other person. This always leads to an escalation of the conflict, and too often, to deadly violence.

The antidote to our counterproductive defensiveness is to stop perceiving others' anger at us as a "threat" to our self-respect. Stop behaving as if our definition of self-respect were: "I'm a worthwhile human being provided no one ever gets angry at me." This is nonsense! The basis of our self-respect is unconditional and is not subject to any proviso. If we are able to remain grounded in a state of self-respect when others get angry at us, our need to "defend" our imaginary perfection does not even arise. We are then in a position to give the other person some relief from THEIR anger. After all, *they* are the one who is in pain and misery. We are in a position to give them some emotional first aid by validating their anger ("I'm sorry that you are so angry at me"). We are not suppressing any counter-anger, or avoiding the other person's grievance, but are putting the confrontation in its appropriate perspective. We are assuming appropriate responsibility for our actions.

Notes

Homework #6: Validate, Validate, Validate!

If you work it right, problems with the other's anger at you can be an opportunity to heal and grow—not just in terms of the relationship, but to grow inside the depths of your own selfhood. First, however, you must transcend your instinctive defense of your ego and validate the other's anger. Validation is "compassion in action." It means you really *feel* for the other person. The other's suffering really stirs your sympathy and empathy: "...I'm sorry you are so angry." You are not just saying it with your mouth; you are speaking from the very depth of your being. What does being "sorry" really mean? It means that your state of *"unawareness"* has been broken. You were doing something unconsciously, asleep—you must have been daydreaming. Something else was on your mind, and by accident, you have stepped on the other's feelings. You *are* sorry about it.

The issue is not who is *right* or who is *wrong*. The issue is that you are willing to cooperate with them; to *resolve* the conflict in a spirit of "mutual" respect ... if *they* are interested. You are not only validating their anger, but secondarily, you are also validating them as being a worthwhile human being in spite of their angry, nasty words and gestures aimed at you. You are validating them in spite of their imperfections and shortcomings. The third validation is for yourself. You have handled the conflict constructively, maturely, like a self-respecting human being. You have also treated the other person with respect and understanding under very difficult circumstances. You have used an anger crisis to make *human* and spiritual progress.

Anger and Miscommunication

Before we continue our examination of the three remaining objects of our anger, something must be said about the role that *miscommunication* plays in the conflicts we have with others, and others have with us. People are continuously in *disputes* and conflict about *everything.* They are in disputes with their husbands, wives, children, friends, and bosses ... *quarreling* is their very style of life! They are simply in a "state" of conflict with others, as well as with THEMSELVES! When there is nobody else to fight with, their violence turns on themselves; they start fighting with themselves. They become self-destructive, they torture themselves, and they become *emotional masochists.* Life is too short to waste in arguments and disputes. Effective communication is the MOST IMPORTANT skill in life.

We spend most of our waking hours talking and communicating with others, but what about LISTENING? What is your capacity to *listen* to and *understand* other people? To deeply understand another human being from that individual's own frame of reference? If you want to interact effectively with others—your wife, your children, your boss, or your neighbor—you need to understand them. And you CANNOT do that without knowing how to listen. The ability to listen—ATTENTIVELY—is the essence of effective human communications. Failure to *effectively* communicate with each other lies at the basis of the majority of the conflict that occurs among us; therefore, we must take a closer look at the role miscommunication and *misunderstanding* play in the process of anger.

One of the greatest problems that impedes our ability to manage anger appropriately is effective communication, how to *say* things so that we are not *misunderstood.* We are misunderstood by others all the time! For example, if the husband is silent too much, if he is

Notes

not talking, and is just sitting quietly minding his own business, suddenly the wife will jump on him! "What is the matter with you? Why are you NOT talking to me? What did I do *now*?" Even our silence cannot be understood correctly by others, is misunderstood by others.

We communicate with each other in many ways. Communications experts say that 70% of our communication with each other is nonverbal. However, we are simply not aware of that nonverbal 70%. The most common form of communication between two human beings is through the use of words ... language. Your wife is saying something to you, but those words are only 30% of the message. The body and other forms of nonverbal communication are also saying something to you, but YOU are not *alert enough*, NOT attentive enough to see them. You simply listened to one or two words and, IMMEDIATELY, you think you have "FULLY" understood what she means! And before she has even completed the sentence, you have already arrived at a conclusion, and are *already prepared* to give her an answer. You have *not* even *listened* to her, and your answer is already prepared! The answer is bound to be "wrong," bound to be simply stupid.

When two persons are talking, just watch their faces. While one person is *saying* something, the other person is preparing to *answer* it; he is NOT listening! *Watch your own conversation!* Is it related to what the other has said? It only APPEARS to be related. You try to make it appear related, but basically, the two of you are like parallel lines: you never intersect, never "intercourse" with each other. Dialogue seems to be going on between you, but it is all just two separate monologues going on simultaneously: You are talking to YOURSELF and the other person is talking to HIMSELF. From a distance, these two monologues simply APPEAR to be a conversation. Yet, even when we listen to each other's words *very* carefully, there is STILL the possibility of misunderstanding occurring.

Words, in any language, are simply "sounds" and then meanings are given to these sounds based on our OWN personal association of ideas with them. Words are nothing more than "phonetic" symbols which have a meaning simply because we have associated these sounds with a certain experience, and if the phonetic symbol is associated again and again with the same experience, we give it a meaning related to that experience. For example, if I see an object and I call it a "chair," and call it that every time I see it, then the word "chair" takes on a meaning and connotation for the "chair" I have seen. However, other people may have used the word "chair" in relation to some OTHER type of object. Therefore, when I say "chair," the other person who hears me DOES NOT understand the same thing! No two persons can have the same "identical" experience of the objects to which we give names; no two persons will have the same meaning for the SAME word! This is the greatest drawback to effective communication with just language ... with just words.

In the case of objects such as chairs, tables, trees, animals, and so on, it is not such a great problem. But when we start talking of things that are "intangible" and of abstract subjects like *love, jealousy, hatred, anger, God, religion, morality, justice*, and so on, the difficulty increases because these words have COMPLETELY DIFFERENT meanings for different people. When two persons are talking about "love," they do NOT realize that they are talking about two different things! Therefore, there is NO way for them to even know that their "understanding" of the word is different! Each will use the word in the sense in which he or she knows it. The listener will "interpret" the word "love" in the sense in which he or

Notes

she understands it! The two of them will have completely different meanings for this same word, and there is no possibility for either of them to know beforehand that his understanding is different from the other.

We know that the connotation given by the association of ideas has to be different since human experience is not identical. Therefore, they cannot possibly have the same meaning! Yet, knowing that the language, the "words" we use cannot possibly mean the same things, we still think communication with words is the MOST effective means of communication. Thus, we continue to experience a lot of conflict based on misunderstandings in our personal and professional relationships with others.

Look deeply into the phenomenon of verbal communication and you will find that, basically, when two persons misunderstand each other, they do so BECAUSE they never understood each other IN THE FIRST PLACE! There was no scope for understanding from the outset. They simply *discover* their misunderstanding the HARD way when they move from the "intangible" to the "tangible," from "words" to reality. When the tangible is brought before them, they will say, "... this is not what I meant!" When we talk of an intangible thing, like love or anger, and when it is "translated" into reality; into some real situation; into an "actual" movement by people toward love or anger, ONLY THEN do we discover the misunderstanding. And, immediately, we try to make the other person "understand" us better by USING MORE WORDS! Ultimately, this only creates more confusion. It is strange to notice that the moment we try to EXPLAIN further, we are simply MORE misunderstood! It would seem to be the other way around, but in fact, if we use FEWER words, the chances of our being misunderstood are actually LESS! The MAJORITY of *"angry misunderstandings"* in our human relationships have arisen from the excessive use of language, of words.

We have been trained ONLY how to talk ... to use words. The result is that we go on creating doubt and confusion (anger) in the minds of the people who are listening to us! We do not know how to communicate from a "deeper" level; how to "feel" ... how to use our "heart." Just "talking more" makes it more difficult, almost impossible, for us to effectively communicate with each other. We see this ALL the time. When you see two persons having a misunderstanding, fighting with each other, hating each other, and when you as a mutual friend intervene and listen to BOTH sides, you discover that it was not either of their fault! It was due to a LACK of communication. There was a *breakdown* in communication; both of them were trying to communicate JUST INTELLECTUALLY—at the level of their intellect.

The more we use just our minds, just our "intellect" (our capacity to use verbal language), the more "uncertain" we are bound to be about the "accuracy" of our communications with others: *"I'm not sure..."*; *"I don't think so..."*; *"perhaps..."*; *"maybe"....* Just listen to the kind of phrases dominating our conversations with others. When we speak in such a way that our *"uncertainties"* are expressly included in our language, then the other person will begin to have "doubts" about our motive, about our *sincerity.* Such expressions show that we are not sure, that we are uncertain about how we feel. And when you are so uncertain in presenting your OWN point of view, there is every reason for the other person to ALSO become uncertain! It creates *fear,* anger, and confusion in the other person: they cannot "trust" you. This is the biggest hurdle in "intellectual" communications. But is there any other way in which we can communicate? If language—

Notes

communication with just words—is not adequate, then how do we overcome these limitations? There is a solution.

Homework #7: Practicing Empathic Listening

There is a "higher" means of communication among human beings, and that is through the use of the *Soul*. Each human being, fortunately, not only has an intellect and mind, but also has that wonderful thing we call the "Soul" or "Spirit." The Soul performs certain functions in consciousness that cannot be performed by the mind and intellect. All of the functions of the mind are "*egocentric*" and limited, and this limitation is what *creates* the difficulties in effective communications among us that we have already explored in some detail.

What does the Soul do that is distinct from the intellect and mind? Our Soul has the ability to become "one" with the other's consciousness. It has the ability to create *empathy* in us. Empathy is the highest peak that our *sympathy* can attain. In "sympathy," you are able to "feel" how the other is feeling. If the other is in pain or misery, is sad or joyous, you can *feel* it. They need not say anything! No words; no language; no explanation of any kind is necessary. Your "heart" gets in *tune* with the other; that is sympathy. It is a kind of symphony of feelings.

However, in a state of "empathy," YOU BECOME ONE with the other! It is not simply a question of getting in tune with the other person. It is "merging," "melting"... it is the experience of your "oneness" with another human being. In fact, there is NO better means of communication among us than through this "spiritual" process of "*emphatic listening*." By emphatic listening, I mean "conscious" *listening* with the intent to UNDERSTAND the other person, to "*move*" into THEIR frame of reference. It is not a question of you agreeing with them; *agreement* is not the issue. The goal of emphatic listening is to deeply, fully understand the other person—emotionally as well as psychologically.

When one is able to use this spiritual function of one's Soul as the *primary* means of communication, there is NO possibility of misunderstanding. There is no miscommunication between you and the other. The ability to "*identify*" oneself with the other is *triggered* and everything becomes clear ... CRYSTAL clear! You will begin to discover the tremendous differences in each of our perceptions of the world and our different ways of orientating reality. Nobody is right and nobody is wrong! You are able to "transcend" the limits of your own individual frame of reference so that you can communicate, deeply, with other people. You no longer take their differences *personally*, as a reflection or invalidation of your own reality, but rather, as an expansion of it! When one is able to communicate at this spiritual level with other people, communication takes place through the "*transference*" of conscious experience! Then, even silence is *communicative*, just holding hands is immensely communicative, a simple glance into each other's eyes is more than enough. *Great understanding* arises; other people NEED not complete their sentence and you have understood them, TRULY understood them! But that is possible only AFTER one has mastered *conscious*, emphatic listening.

Select a relationship in which you sense a "high" level of conflict. WRITE down the situation and try to understand it from the other person's point of view. In your next

Notes

encounter with the person, "consciously" focus your attention on what they are saying—not with just their words: *Listen attentively* to the "spaces" between their words; listen with your *"third ear"* to the silences in between their speech. See, with an opened *"third"* eye, their gestures and body language. Look and listen to UNDERSTAND them, then compare what you are hearing and seeing with what you wrote down. How accurate were your previous *assumptions*? Had you REALLY understood them? Once this level of *"emphatic"* awareness becomes rooted, the level of conflicts with others arising out of misunderstanding simply disappears into thin air. Now, let us continue our examination of the remaining objects of our anger.

Object #3 — Managing Our Anger at Self

The most important relationship we will ever have is the relationship with ourselves. If one part of us is in "conflict" with some other part of us, we cannot expect to be happy. And if we have failed to develop a healthy relationship with ourselves, we will not, *by definition*, be capable of developing a healthy relationship with others.

As children, our parents and teachers' over-critical remarks led us to believe that our "human" faults and imperfections were the source of their "disappointment" with us. They gave us *perfectionist* ideals to fulfill (which were impossible), and our inability to live up to their "standards" was proof of our worthlessness. This has created a tremendous sense of guilt that we are somehow NOT what we "should" be; that something is "wrong" with us; that we are *inferior*. This feeling of being "worthless" and inferior BECAUSE of our faults and imperfections is called "self-contempt." It is the exact opposite of self-respect.

The striving for perfection is the root cause of our anger at ourselves. We strive for perfection in order to "prove" we are not worthless, and when we ULTIMATELY *fail* to be perfect, we get angry at *ourselves*! Nobody can be perfect; nobody needs to be perfect. How can one be perfect in an imperfect world? Because of our mistaken ambitions to be perfect—which we carry over from our childhood—we are driving ourselves (and others) crazy! Nobody is *born* insane, but is driven insane by the pursuit of perfection. We have all been trying for years to be perfect, and there are only two possible outcomes of our efforts.

One is you will simply become *neurotic*. Since you cannot become perfect, you will become burdened with a mountain of guilt. Sooner or later, the weight of this guilt will crush you. It will destroy all the joy in your life; it will poison your happiness and not allow you to celebrate life. You will ultimately become suicidal. The second possibility is you will become a *hypocrite*. You will go on *"pretending to be perfect,"* but that will just be a facade, a mask. Hiding behind the mask, you will simply remain the same old imperfect person. Both are ugly phenomena. Going crazy, becoming neurotic, becoming guilt-ridden, becoming suicidal, becoming a lying hypocrite—all of these are the ugly, sickening consequences of mismanaged anger at our own imperfections and shortcomings.

Anger at ourselves, self-contempt, creates an intense and painful state of inner turmoil and conflict. We become intensely self-critical, self-condemning, and self-punishing. We become our *own worst enemy*. We then will try to relieve the pain of our self-contempt in many ways. We will try to "lose" ourselves in order to lose the pain. We will try to escape from ourselves into drugs, alcohol, food, sex, and so on. In fact, many people will even

Notes

escape into some form of *mental illness* and become psychotic or schizophrenic. Until we are able to reconcile with and accept ourselves, shortcomings and all, we are destined to eventually become mentally and emotionally ill. One has just to be oneself. The moment we accept ourselves *as we are*, all burdens—mountainous burdens of guilt—simply disappear. Then life becomes sheer joy!

Homework #8: Just Be Yourself

Self-comparison is a social disease, because we are taught from the very beginning to compare ourselves with others. In trying to find our place in our family of origin, as a child we often compared ourselves unfavorably with an older brother or sister. We may have despaired in not being as "intelligent" or as "strong" or "good looking" as our sibling. We may have become discouraged very early in life with ourselves and resigned to a lifetime of being "stupid" or "weak" or the "ugly duckling" of the family. The destructive and discouraging effects of this unfavorable comparison are even more damaging if we have compared ourselves unfavorably to a YOUNGER sibling! Later on, our mother or father started comparing us with the neighbor's children; our teachers started comparing us with the other students; and so on.

From the very beginning you were being told to "compare" yourself with others. And, by and by, you started to feel inferior. This constellation of feelings of inferiority, guilt, and self-anger, in a context of self-contempt, can lay the foundation for a lifetime of depression, discouragement, and self-destruction. Self-comparison is a "killer" disease; it is like a cancer that destroys your very Soul until it ultimately kills all your self-respect. Each individual is unique; no comparison is possible. You are just yourself as the other person is just himself. It is very important for our mental health that we do not fall into this trap of self-recrimination.

Do you compare a lily to a rose? You do not compare an apple to an orange! You know they are different and that no comparison is possible, nor is it even needed. They BOTH are appreciated for what they are. Each has its own unique flavor and texture; neither is "better" than the other. Do not compare yourself with others. Comparison will create all kinds of mental problems for you. If you fall into the trap of comparison, naturally you will become either very egotistical and start "tripping," or you will become discouraged, bitter, and depressed. It depends on whom you are comparing yourself with. If you are comparing yourself with people who are in some way greater than you are, you will become very bitter and depressed. Or, if you are comparing yourself with someone who is in some way smaller or lesser than you are, you will become very egotistic, very vain.

If you do not compare, then you are neither bigger nor smaller, neither ugly nor beautiful, neither intelligent nor stupid: you are simply yourself! *As you are*, you are perfect—including your faults! You do not belong to any hierarchy. Nobody is higher than you are, and nobody is lower than you are—because nobody is like you. Hence, no comparison is possible; competition is simply futile. In a state of JUST BEING YOURSELF—in a *deep* acceptance of yourself—a deep gratitude toward life springs up inside you, and all of your inner turmoil will simply disappear.

Notes

Object #4 — Anger at the Absent Other

One of the most difficult kinds of anger to manage is the anger we have at people who are no longer a part of our life. It could be a spouse we have divorced or who has divorced us years ago, and yet we are STILL angry at them. You may have loved some man or woman and they never responded to you. They are no longer involved with you—or even want to be involved with you. You really loved the person, but have not understood that there was no *necessity* for the other person to love you in return. You are still "clinging" to your resentment of being "wronged" by them. You keep playing with your wound. You are a *masochist*. I will not say you are a fool; you are simply a "closet" masochist. You are creating your own torture, your own anguish, by holding on to your anger. You are playing the "victim" game—the game of being a "martyr." You are enjoying your "crucifixion"; you have become "obsessed" with it. Obsession is simply a wound in your psyche that goes on demanding your attention. You cannot drop it. It is *your* wound. You have nurtured it from its infancy, so how can you just drop it? How do we give ourselves some relief from this "residual" anger we carry over from our past relationships? The person we are angry at is no longer present, they are "absent" in our life ... perhaps even dead. How do we resolve our anger issues with them?

Homework #9: The Anger Letter

One way to solve our *residual* anger at the absent other is to write our anger down on a piece of paper. At first glance, this seems too simplistic to be of any value. Yet this technique is very powerful when done the right way. You are not writing a "hate" letter. Rather, by writing you are making yourself more conscious, more aware of the anger. Writing helps you to "see" into the nature of your anger, to begin to understand it; to pay "right" attention to it; to be "meditative" toward it. And the more consciousness and meditativeness your writing is able to create in you, the quicker your residual anger is healed. The writing becomes a healing force; it becomes a powerful form of anger therapy.

Writing down our feelings and thoughts connected with our past conflicts triggers a process of catharsis. Old ideas and attitudes from the past become accessible and can be reexamined; we can now see them with "fresh" eyes. Slowly, the writing begins to become an energy phenomenon. Many emotions that were suppressed begin to uncoil; to start coming up, bubbling up. Emotional energy starts being released. Suddenly, you will start crying, really sobbing. After this "deep" crying, you will feel relieved—as if a burden of a thousand pounds has finally disappeared. Your tears have arisen from a deep level of "understanding" and truthfulness. You will feel weightless; you will feel more at ease about the old incidents, much calmer about it all.

If the writing is rooted in the truth—if you are truthfully saying what made you the most angry about the incident; how it made you feel about yourself—if you are not just making a laundry list of complaints and criticism against the other person, then you will feel rejuvenated after finishing the anger letter. Slowly, your wound begins to heal. Slowly, the residual anger loses its grip on you. You will see it start to transform into a positive, rather than negative, energy; into *compassion* rather than *hatred* for the other person. This is the *miracle* of "awareness": it can transform any emotional energy into its polar OPPOSITE!

Notes

Try to hate somebody "consciously" and you will discover that it simply cannot be done! It is impossible. Either consciousness is not there, and then you can hate; or consciousness is there, and you are unable to hate. They both cannot exist simultaneously. Consciousness and hatred, light and darkness—both cannot exist in you at the same time. Your hatred is nothing but the absence of consciousness, the absence of awareness. Writing the anger letter will create a new level of awareness inside you. You will feel very, very alive after writing it; somehow younger than before, as if YEARS have disappeared. You will feel livelier, fresher. But if you have just been writing bullshit—if you were just doing it half-heartedly, mechanically—afterwards, you will feel tired, "wasted." You were unnecessarily wasting your time and energy, avoiding the truth.

These anger letters do not have to be mailed to the person. That's optional. We are not writing our anger letter in order to get revenge or punish the other person's "conscience"; to make them feel guilty and ashamed. We write our anger letters in order to give *ourselves* some relief from *our own* distress. If we are still angry at a deceased loved one, a parted lover or an old friend, at God, at life, at "society" or even at ourselves, we can choose to write our anger down on paper instead of holding it inside us. Afterwards, we can file it, mail it, or tear it up—that is also our choice. The homework is finished! This technique also works well for managing the next and last object of anger, "abstract" anger.

Object #5 — *Managing Abstract/Cosmic Anger*

At some time or other, we have all become angry at "life"; angry about some event or circumstance in life that has caused us a great deal of pain, a great deal of suffering. It may have been the premature and unexpected death of a loved one; the sudden loss of our health from an accident; a financial or natural disaster; or a thousand and one other of life's uncontrollable catastrophes. The common affect they each have on us is pain; a great suffering and a feeling of "cosmic injustice" arise within us: *"Why me?* I didn't deserve this suffering, this pain, this disaster. This is *unfair* ... life is unfair to me!" This feeling of cosmic injustice, in turn, creates "cosmic" anger in us. The object of our anger is no longer some specific person. It is not aimed at any particular "human" agency; it is "abstract." Its target is intangible and invisible: the "unseen" and "unknowable" cause that directs and controls the world events impacting our daily lives. Our anger is "existential"... we are angry at existence, period!

Homework #10: Accept Life

The only antidote for healing the "spiritual agony" of our abstract/cosmic anger is to develop the ability to "adapt" to reality; to accept life's terms and learn to cope with its crises. Life is made of both good and bad experiences, of pain and pleasure. *"Ais dhammo sanatano"*—that's the way life is. Our vicissitudes provide us with an opportunity to grow. When something terrible happens, one should never flee into denial or escape into self-pity; one has to go through it. That is how one grows. Never try to avoid life's challenges. One has to respond to the challenge and go into it. That is what being responsible means: the capacity and ability to "respond" to reality (respons-ability). Never try to escape; never try to

Notes

dodge life. Spinoza says, "Do not get angry, do not cry, simply understand." *Ais dhammo sanatano*. Trying to avoid the challenges of life is what keeps so many people juvenile.

"Living" requires courage. Anybody can "exist," but existence is not the same as living. *Living* only occurs within the context of courage, and *courage* means going into the unknown in spite of your fears; in spite of your suffering. Courage does *not* mean fearlessness. *Fearlessness* happens when you go on being courageous. It is the ultimate outcome of courage. The fears and the suffering are there, but if you go on accepting the challenges of life, adapting to its reality, slowly the fear and suffering disappear. The experience of the joy that the unknown brings ... the thrill and "adventure" of life, makes you strong enough to go forward.

The whole point is: *Accept life as it is*, and do not try to avoid its ups and downs. To do that, is to attempt the impossible. Against reality, your foolish ambitions will *always* fail. Expecting your life to be "problem-free" is a *negative ambition*. It is a *personal conflict* with reality and a conflict with just plain common sense. In fact, your "problems" are created by *you*. Situations and events are there, true; they are "real." But your problems are not there; they are not a part of existence. *Your problems* are your *interpretations* of the situation or event. The same situation or event may not be a problem for any other person; it is a problem only for YOU. Problems are subjective, so it depends on you. You can *create* a problem out of something or not—it is up to you—but the problem *itself* does *not* exist; it is not a part of existence. It only exists, psychologically, in *your own mind*.

Look closely at it the next time you become obsessed with a problem. When you start "tripping," just stand back and look at the "problem." Is it "really" there? Is it objectively a part of reality? Or have you simply created it? Look deeply into it, and you will suddenly see it begin to disappear; it will become smaller and smaller. The more you are able to focus your awareness on it, the faster it begins to shrink, to lose its intensity. Ultimately, it will simply evaporate into thin air. It simply "dissolves" ... it is no longer there; and then you will simply laugh about it.

Remember, NO problem can EVER be "solved." How can you solve something that does not exist? This will only create MORE problems for you! Your problems do not need to be solved by you; they simply need to be understood. This simple truth about the nature of life's problems, once understood, is enough to transform your life. Just a clear understanding that your abstract anger has its foundation in your "cosmic ignorance" immediately releases you from the spiritual agony of your abstract and cosmic anger. This knowledge, once grasped, will transform you, liberate you, and save your Soul.... *Ais dhammo sanatano*. Meditate on it.

Notes

Part Three

The Fundamentals of Anger Management

When it comes to managing anger, there are basic facts everyone must know. These are facts we did not learn in school because no one ever taught them. We have been limping along without them all our lives.

- **Anger is an emotional response to a grievance.** The grievance can be real or imagined; it can be past, present, or future; it can be rational or irrational; but it makes us angry just the same.

- **Anger is painful.** Our impulse is to relieve the pain of our anger one way or another. If we do not know how to relieve our pain the right way, we are liable to relieve it the wrong way, which will only make it worse.

- **Our anger at the grievance creates a problem for us.** We want to relieve the pain of our grievance but we do not know how. We make up a solution that sounds like it ought to work, but it cannot be successful if it was not a product of our rational thought processes. For many of us, those mature processes are too slow and boring. To save time, we fall back on immature attitudes from our past: "This should do the trick." We overreact, we lash out. We get revenge in the name of justice and fair play. We carry grudges. We become mean and spiteful. These are all behaviors arising out of anger attitudes. Our attitudes have no brains. They may save us a lot of time up front, but they cost us a bundle in the future. This approach to saving time is an example of a non-solution that makes things worse instead of better.

- **We call these non-solutions "good intentions":** "I meant well, it just didn't turn out that way!" Our good intentions are always

    ➤ Self-indulgent, self-serving.
    ➤ Counterproductive.
    ➤ Self-destructive.

- **The antidote to good intentions is a *real* intention.** In a real intention, we use our mature judgment to tell us what the situation requires us to do and that is what we do—no more, no less.

- **When we do something that reality does *not* require us to do, we call that mischief.** It doesn't need to be done. It makes things worse for everybody. Good intentions are a form of mischief.

- **We make mischief because it is exciting.** We holler and scream, we swear, we beat people up, we drive like lunatics. This is not positive, happy excitement. It is negative, self-destructive excitement.

- **One purpose of our exciting mischief is to relieve the pain of our unresolved anger and our self-doubt.** This mindless, well-intentioned solution will fail.

Notes

- **When we fail to solve a problem in childhood, we often take it personally.** We cannot respect someone who fails, especially ourselves. We take the failure *as if it were a reflection on our worth as a person.* In other words, we sink into feelings of worthlessness, good-for-nothing, inferiority, and inadequacy to cope. As a consequence of these setbacks, we develop attitudes toward ourselves, toward others, and toward life.

- **An attitude is a predisposition to behave in a certain way.** When there is a difficult, stressful situation, it becomes a problem we cannot solve. Our negative attitudes kick in and make us behave in ways that are not in our own best interests. We become angry at ourselves for our stupid behavior, but it was not stupid. It had nothing to do with intelligence. It arose out of attitudes, not our mature judgment.

- **These feelings and attitudes toward ourselves are painful.** We do not know how to solve the problem of feeling worthless either! Our pain becomes deeper and deeper.

- **We call this pain "self-contempt."** When we do not know how to relieve our self-contempt, we try to escape from it into criticizing, complaining, moralizing, punishing, and controlling in ways that do not work. These are all more self-defeating, self-destructive good intentions that we have for ourselves.

- **Since we do not know the name of our pain from the past, we cannot relieve it in the right way.** No one tells us what the antidote is. They tell us to "try harder" or "grow up." These are insulting good intentions. They are mischief. They do not help. They discourage us. They make things worse.

- **Their good intentions make us angry.** Then they punish us for becoming angry. That makes our original anger worse. Their punishment was another counterproductive good intention on their part. Everybody loses.

- **We feel like a victim, out of control. We are angry at the unfairness, the wrongness.** We become sensitized to the unfairness and wrongness all around us. We may acquire the attitude that it is our responsibility to right these wrongs, and we set out to try. Or we may give up in discouragement and stop trying. Either way, our negative attitudes keep us from living our lives on a mature, independent basis.

- **Our negative attitudes set us up to focus on the negative, anger-producing aspect of life.** We are too busy with these insoluble fairness problems to enjoy the happiness that others seem to be enjoying.

- **We may acquire the attitude that "Helpers don't help me.** I cannot trust anyone to help me. I must keep my problems to myself. I have to solve them all by myself, but I don't know how!" We take pride in our imaginary self-reliance, which is no more than overcompensation for our self-contempt.

- **People who have self-contempt do not deserve to be happy and successful.** They do not deserve to be First Best. They deserve only to be First Worst. They may strive to be Number One in positive ways, and even succeed at first. But their old attitude toward what they deserve will rise up and predispose them to behave

Notes

negatively. If left untreated, this attitude that they do not deserve happiness will bring about the downfall that they have deserved all along.

- **The antidote to self-contempt is self-respect.** This is the feeling that one is a worthwhile human being in spite of one's faults and imperfections.

- **On this basis of our self-worth, we deserve to succeed.** As self-respecting people we are not driven to succeed; we are free to succeed, no more and no less than anyone else is.

- **We deserve to live and be happy,** to love and be loved, to belong as an equal member of the human race, not because we are perfect, but in spite of the fact that we are not.

- **Attitudes determine behavior.** If we do not respect ourselves, if we hold ourselves worthless and inferior, we will try to relieve our pain by

  ➤ overcompensating for our feelings of inferiority;

  ➤ making self-destructive, self-indulgent mischief at home, at work, and anywhere else we can get away with it;

  ➤ having our own good intentions to straighten out or punish those fellow human beings who have had the misfortune to cross our path;

  ➤ escaping from our pain into self-indulgent, negative excitement;

  ➤ escaping from our pain into self-destructive addictive behavior;

  ➤ bringing about the disaster that worthless people deserve; and

  ➤ mismanaging our anger and making our lives more painful and complicated than they need to be.

- **In addition to the external stresses of everyday life, negative attitudes can cause us to suffer from internal stresses and strains** that make our lives worse instead of better. These internal stresses bring about mental and emotional problems such as anxiety, obsessive thinking, and depression, and physical, health problems such as high blood pressure, stroke, ulcers, and other "stress-related" diseases.

- **We can replace our negative attitudes with positive ones.** We can accomplish this replacement process by doing our Homework when life presents us with an opportunity to do so. Instead of displacing anger onto someone who doesn't deserve it, we can choose to ask ourselves an anger question: "Who am I *really* angry at?" The answer may surprise us. We may still be angry at a cruel father. We may be angry that we lost our mother when we were six years old, or that our parents divorced and broke our heart.

- **Who else am I angry at?** If we peel the layers of our anger still further, we often find that we are angry at ourselves without even knowing it. We cannot relieve the pain of these underlying angers if we do not know they are down there.

- **We can choose to write out our anger.** The next step in the Homework process would be to write an anger letter to the persons who caused us the grief or loss. We may never deliver it. Writing it is for *us*, not them. We can catch ourselves saying

Notes

things like, "But it wasn't their fault. I have no right to be angry." It is not a matter of guilt or fault or blame. It is a matter of human imperfection. It was our parent's human imperfections that created a painful problem that we didn't know how to solve. As an adult, we can solve it now by writing our pain and grief out of our system onto a piece of paper in the present. We are in control. We are making a choice on our own independent terms. We are making it happen right now. We will feel relief from the pressure, tension, and stress that mismanaged anger has been causing. If we are angry at ourselves, we can write ourselves an anger letter. Be sure to call your anger by its rightful name. You are not upset, you are *angry*.

- **The next stage in the process is forgiveness, which is a letting go of anger.** It is not denying what they did or condoning it. It is not a matter of right and wrong. Their negative behavior caused you a painful grievance, and you are doing something constructive to relieve your own pain. You are making another choice in your own behalf: to let your anger and pain go. It is for *your* benefit, not theirs.

- **The next step is self-respect.** You have used an anger situation as a way of replacing your old self-doubt with self-respect on a realistic basis. You have solved a problem, you have assumed appropriate responsibility for yourself. You have experienced relief, accomplishment, and positive success in your own behalf. You have made it happen. You have let it go the right way. That is positive control. You have earned the right to feel like a worthwhile human being in spite of your faults and imperfections.

Notes

Glossary of Terms

Acceptance vs. Resignation

Acceptance is taking life as it comes; resignation is giving up in discouragement.

Allergic to Happiness

The consequence of the unself-respecting person's attitude of unworthiness to be happy. The individual lives in fear that happiness will end in disaster. To prevent disaster, he or she arranges to avoid happiness or sabotage it. Their attitude is that, "It hurts less if I do it to myself."

Anger

An emotional response to a grievance, whether real or imaginary; whether past, present, or future; or whether to oneself or one's group. The grievance may be rational or non-rational, but its pain is still real.

Angerphobia

The fear of expressing or even experiencing one's legitimate anger. The fear may be of
- displeasing;
- being rejected, abandoned;
- losing control;
- being victimized; or
- being annihilated.

Anxiety

A feeling of dread; the expectation that something terrible is going to happen in the future and feeling out of control in the meantime. We feel out of control when we
- live on other people's terms;
- live in the future;
- "control" our anger in ways that do not work; and
- "control" our lives in ways that do not work. (See "Controlness")

Attitude

A predisposition to behave in a certain way. (See "Glossary of Attitudes")

Belonging

The feeling that one is an equal member of the human race, no more, no less than anyone else is. Prerequisite: Belonging to oneself on an appropriate basis: "I belong to myself. There is a self here to belong to."

Control

Taking life as it comes and making things happen that need to happen.

Notes

Controlness	The unself-respecting person's tendency to define control as if it meant • preventing disaster before it happens; • knowing what other people are thinking; • knowing how to solve every problem; or • knowing what is going to happen in the future. When these conditions are not met, the individual feels out of control. Since these impossible conditions cannot be met, the individual feels out of control much of the time. The out-of-controlness may be experienced as anxiety, obsessive thinking, or depression arising out of anger at the self for failing to control "well enough," that is, perfectly. The individual's attitude is, "I should have seen that coming. It is my fault that I did not. 1 am angry at myself!"
Courage	The willingness to take a risk.
Discouragement	The absence of courage; the unwillingness to take a risk.
Displaced Anger	Anger that is directed at a safer target than the individual who caused the grievance.
Fairness	Using our adult judgment to treat others without bias according to the needs of the reality situation.
"Fairnessness"	Defining fairness as if it meant, "Getting my way!"
Frustration	Feeling angry plus powerlessness and out of control.
Good Enough	The attitude that, "As good as I am right now, that's good enough. If I am better still tomorrow, that's all right, too." The mistake is to worry about it. (See "Self-respect")
"Good for Nothing" Syndrome	The feeling that one's "goodness" is not appreciated, therefore, one is "worthless." The individual is dependent on the validation of others for his or her worth as a person. They are angry at themselves for being "good" in the first place. They feel "stupid" and out of control. There is nothing they can do about it. This syndrome is often a contributor to depression.
Good Intentions	Making up solutions that sound good when we really don't know what reality requires us to do. (See "Overcompensation," "Mischief")

Notes

Guilt vs. Regret	Guilt has to do with the legal consequence of perpetrating a crime. Regret is the wish that things were other than they are, but they are not. We are not guilty of a crime. It is merely regrettable. We are not worthless. We are worthwhile in spite of it.
"I Want My Way" Syndrome	The attitude that one's worth as a person is defined in terms of getting one's way. Not getting one's way is painful. It triggers attitudes from the past, such as: • "It's unfair." • "I am unloved." • "It's wrong." • "I feel abandoned." The intensity of the desire to "get" is directly proportional to the pain of "not getting." The issue, then, is not the object of desire. The issue is that the getter wants his way in order to relieve the pain of not getting it.
Managing Anger	Using one's adult judgment to express anger appropriately in the middle ground between the extremes of super anger and suppression. For example: • "It makes me angry when you do that!" • *No one can make you angry but yourself!* • "I didn't get this way all by myself ... I had help!" Writing an anger letter or drawing a picture can also provide appropriate relief from the pain of anger. "Working it off" gives temporary distraction but does not address the grievances that originally provoked the anger.
"Marlboro Man" Syndrome	One who takes pride in having no feelings from the neck up or down. This is not a sign of "manly" strength. This syndrome arises out of fear of being found vulnerable, being victimized and losing control. (See "Controlness," "Overcompensation," "Self-contempt")
Mischief	That which does not need to be done. Mischief-making is characteristic of unself-respecting people.
Obsessing	A mental/emotional syndrome that occurs when we have an insoluble problem that we feel we must solve perfectly. Nothing less will do. We are out of control until we "solve" this insoluble problem which, of course, we cannot do. It is a consequence of mistaken definitions of control in a context of self-doubt or self-contempt.

39

Notes

Overcompensation	The attitude that one must strive to prove that one is not worthless by attaining "good enoughness," that is, perfection. It is a set up for failure and self-anger. The inevitable failure serves to confirm the individual's self-contempt.
"The Pleasing" Syndrome	Playing a role on other people's terms for fear of displeasing them and being punished, rejected, abandoned, or victimized. The antidote is to "Do what pleases *you*." This gives the individual an experience of accomplishment, success, control, living in the present, liberation from old roles and attitudes, independence, and appropriate responsibility for one's own well being. It replaces the old pleasing role with a mature identity, and the attitude that one deserves to be happy, no more and no less than anyone else.
Real Intentions	Using our judgment to tell us what reality requires us to do, and then having the courage to do it.
Revenge	The attempt to relieve the pain of our anger by hurting others as they have hurt us. This tendency is based on an immature definition of fairness from childhood. It is an example of overcompensation: building ourselves up by tearing others down. Revenge is not the product of mature thought processes. It arises out of non-rational negative attitudes from the past, attitudes toward ourselves, such as: • "I am entitled to even the score." • "I am entitled to exemption from the consequences of my destructive behavior" toward others. • "Bad people deserve to be taught a lesson for their own good" and toward civilization. • "The wheels of justice turn too slow for me. That's for wimps, anyway. I prefer my own superior brand of justice." Revenge promises more than it delivers.
"Reverse Fairness"	Treating others better than they deserve to be treated. (See "'The Pleasing' Syndrome," "Good Intentions," "Overcompensation")
Self-contempt	a. The feeling that one is inadequate, inferior, and worthless and is therefore unworthy of happiness, success, or love. b. The absence of self-respect.

Notes

Self-respect	The feeling that one is a worthwhile human being in spite of one's faults and imperfections. It is an attitude that we have toward ourselves. It enables us to bounce back when we have taken something personally.
Selfishness	Taking without giving. Very often, one has the attitude that, "What I have to give is worthless. It is not worth giving. It would only be rejected anyway, so why bother?" What does that leave? It leaves "taking."
Stress	The consequence of exceeding one's ability to adapt. Stress can be relieved by • reducing the external sources of stress; • relieving the internal stress caused by mismanaged anger and self-contempt; and/or • improving one's competence to take life as it comes. Major sources of internal stress are • our inadequacy to manage our legitimate anger appropriately; • our predisposition to take reversals more personally than we need to take them; and • our predisposition to control in non-rational ways.
Super Anger	Feeling angrier than one needs to feel as a consequence of unresolved anger from the past.
Suppressed Anger	Anger that is kept inside for fear of the consequences of expressing it; often confused with "control." (See "Anger-phobia")
Undercompensation	Doing less than one is able to do because of discouragement, fear of success, fear of failure, or fear of humiliating exposure of one's inadequacy to cope. (See "Self-contempt")

Notes

"The Victimizer" Syndrome   The victimizer is one who solves problems by tearing others down. Victimizers often perceive victimization where no victimization is intended. They are angry at the perceived "grievance" and feel "entitled" to take the law into their own hands. They feel exempt from the consequences of their own negative behavior. They are able to justify their behavior to themselves as "righting a wrong." They are often displacing anger from the past onto vulnerable victims in the present. The victimization is their self-serving attempt to "relieve" the pain of their anger and self-contempt. Since this "solution" to the problem cannot succeed, the victimizer must keep trying forever.

Notes

Glossary of Attitudes

We need absurd words to capture the flavor of these inappropriate carryovers from our childhood. Seeing them as absurd helps us to loosen their grip on our daily lives.

Expectanciness	The tendency to live up or down to the expectations of others. Self-respecting people are more likely to trust their own judgments and values and to behave independently. People who doubt their worth as persons are more vulnerable to living in terms of the judgments, expectations, and prejudices of others.
Fairnessness	The absurd expectation that life is supposed to be fair to us (but not necessarily anyone else). We become angry when this attitude toward life is dis-confirmed by the ups and downs of everyday life in an imperfect world. As a consequence, we are going to be angry most of the time.
Faultophobia	Fear of guilt, fault, and blame. This attitude predisposes us to blame everyone but ourselves for our own shortcomings. The individual is already so filled with feelings of guilt and failure that he cannot tolerate any more. On a deeper level, the individual is striving for perfection. Any guilt, fault, or blame would constitute a flaw in his makeup and preclude the attainment of his unrealistic, overcompensatory goal.
Faultophilia	Accepting inappropriate guilt, fault, and blame as a way of confirming one's preexisting conviction of worthlessness. To this individual, the role of the "guilty party, the victim, or the scapegoat," etc. is preferable to the even worse alternative of having no role at all!
Faultophrenia	The mistaken attitude that the issue is guilt, fault, or blame. Most of the time, fixing guilt does not solve the problem, repair the damage, or prevent a recurrence. Faultfinding is a useless good intention that often misses the point. The issue is imperfection. The remedy is to replace self-doubt with self-respect.
Humilitude	Taking excessive pride in one's extreme humility: "When it comes to humility, I'm tops."

Notes

Moneyphobia	The attitude that money is evil and contaminates one's personal purity and nobility. Besides, it might make one happy, and that is exactly what unself-respecting people do not deserve to be. a. Using money and material considerations to control others to their own detriment. b. A substitute for happiness on the part of people who don't deserve any.
Moral Insanity	Overcompensation for feelings of personal and moral inferiority by escaping into a fictitious, self-appointed moral superiority over one's imperfect fellow human beings. (See "Moralitosis")
Moralitosis	The delusion that one is specially qualified to stand in moral judgment upon other members of the human race. (See "Overcompensation")
Rationalitosis	a. The delusion that our behavior and ideas are supremely rational and not driven by attitudes from the past. b. The delusion that non-rational problems can be solved rationally. c. The mistaken attitude that the non-rational aspects of the human condition are not worthy of serious consideration unless they can be measured to the fourth decimal place.

Responsibility	The willingness to contribute one's fair share toward accomplishing that which needs to be done.
	a. Super-responsibility: Assuming more responsibility than reality requires us to assume. (See "Overcompensation")
	b. Under-responsibility: The unwillingness to assume one's fair share of the work to be done due to
	  1. fear of failure, or
	  2. fear of humiliating exposure.
	This syndrome is often misdiagnosed as "laziness."

Smartitude	The delusion that one is smarter than one is: "I knew that!" (See "Overcompensation")
Stubbornness	The consequence of foolishly staking one's self-respect on the outcome of a dispute. The issue of the dispute is not the issue. The issue is the *fear* of losing one's self-worth as one has mistakenly defined it.

Notes

Stupiditude

a. The attitude that one is not smart enough.
b. The conviction that one is stupid because:
One does not know everything in the world.
One has failed to predict the future.
One has failed to read another's mind.

Wrongophobia

Anger at "wrongness" that must be stamped out totally and perfectly, no matter how much it hurts the other person. (See "Good Intentions," "Moral Insanity")

Notes

Relieve Your Anger

1. How am I feeling right now?

____Anxiety	____Worthless	____Hostile	____Depressed
____Mean/evil	____Revengeful	____Bitchy	____Bitter
____Rebellious	____Paranoid	____Victimized	____Numb
____Sarcastic	____Resentful	____Frustrated	____Destructive

These are some of the names that we give to our feelings of anger! There is no cure for any of them. The first step in resolving our anger problem is to **identify** it as anger! The purpose of this step is to make our anger more specific. No one can manage anger that is vague and covered up with euphemisms.

2. What happened to make you angry?

If we can focus on the specific incident that triggered our anger, our anger becomes more understandable and easier to manage.

_____

_____

_____

_____

_____

_____

3. Who am I angry at?

____My own self	____My spouse	____My partner	____My boss
____The kids	____God	____The human race	____My life
____All men	____All women	____Other races	____Miscellaneous

Our anger usually will involve five (5) general areas: (1) our anger at others, (2) others' anger at us, (3) our anger at self, (4) residual anger from the past, or (5) abstract anger.

Now that you have established the fact that you are angry and that your anger has an "object" in the real world, you are ready for the fourth step in working through the anger process. You are ready to factor your anger into its main components. If you can **identify** the specific facets of your anger, you will be in a better position to put your anger into a more moderate and manageable perspective. You can do this by asking yourself a series of focusing questions.

Notes

4. How did the situation make me feel besides angry?

(Example #1: I resent being forced to give in to them all the time. It makes me feel powerless!)

(Example #2: His criticisms of me make me feel unappreciated and good for nothing.)

_____

_____

_____

_____

_____

Now that you have pinpointed your feelings underlying your anger, you are ready to put your anger in a clearer perspective. The next step is to "peel" your anger down to the next layer.

5. What about this angers me the most?

For example, you have established the fact that in the above situation it made you feel powerless, unappreciated, or good for nothing. You are now ready to take a closer look at these feelings underlying your anger. What is it about being made to feel powerless that angers you the most? Some examples of what you might find upon deeper analysis is:

- "There is nothing that I can do about it."
- "I feel so stupid!"
- "I feel guilty for allowing it to happen."
- "I feel inadequate to cope with this situation."

Having peeled your anger down to this level, you are now ready to penetrate your anger at its deepest level. You are ready to focus on the real issue underlying all of the prior layers and levels of your emotional distress.

6. Now, what about this angers me the MOST?

This level of self-analysis usually brings us down to the bedrock, down to the fundamental issue that underlies all the others, and that must be identified and relieved if we are to strengthen our vulnerability to mismanaging our anger—and making our lives more miserable than they need to be. The answer found at this level of self-analysis often turns out to be, "I feel so worthless!" It is hard for us to respect someone who is stupid, helpless, inadequate, and powerless! And when we have those feelings toward ourselves, they destroy our respect for our own selves.

Notes